MIND: Unlocked

AF624564

Teâ Bollen

BookLeaf Publishing

MIND: Unlocked © 2022 Teâ Bollen

All rights reserved.

No part of this publication may be reproduced, stored in a retrieval system, or transmitted, in any form or by any means, electronic, mechanical, photocopying, recording or otherwise, without the prior written permission of the presenters.

Teâ Bollen asserts the moral right to be identified as author of this work.

Presentation by *BookLeaf Publishing*

Web: www.bookleafpub.com

E-mail: info@bookleafpub.com

ISBN: 9789357210300

First edition 2022

DEDICATION

I dedicate this book of poems to anyone who has or had struggles with mental health.

No minds are the same. We deal with our battles in different ways. Our battles themselves are not the same. We can find similarities in the battles others face, but we are all valid with the emotions we have.

If you are in need of help, please reach out to someone you trust. Know that help if always there if you want to ask for it.

Numbers For Support:

- Shout (text shout) - 85258

- Samaritans - 116 123

- SANEline - 0300 304 7000

- The National Suicide Prevention Helpline UK - 0800 689 5652

There are many more you can contact, so please ask for help.

ACKNOWLEDGEMENT

Firstly, I would like to thank the readers for purchasing my debut poetry book. I like to think that the poems connect myself to the readers that relate. Even if the readers don't relate to my poems, that's perfectly fine too. Since this book is circulated around mental health, which means any struggles the readers face connect us that way. Battles don't need to be the same to be relatable. I thank all my readers for supporting my work and I hope that this can be a small step to showing mental health is just as important as physical health.

Also, I would like to thank the people who have and continue to support me;

The mental health professionals who didn't give up on me when I wanted to give up on myself.

Leoni, who was and is the best person to help and support me through the days when I didn't want to leave my bed. Always manages to make me smile and for that I am so thankful.

My closest friends. Beth & Sophie. Who I don't see all that much these days but they are always there to listen and help in anyway they can. I thank them for all the times I unloaded my stresses to them and they would just hug me. I will always be there for you two like you have been for me.

My first ISVA (Independent Sexual Violence Advisor), Emily. As well as my current ISVA, Lauren. Who have both supported me during the process of reporting one of the worst experiences of my life. The continued support of aiding me in moving forward and healing from that incident is something I am so grateful for.

My secondary school English teacher, who pushed me to excel in creative writing. They saw something in my writing that I didn't even know existed. They told me I could do great things with the way I write using so much feeling and emotion is captivating. Thank you.

And lastly to BookLeaf Publishing, for giving me this opportunity to put my work out into the world for anyone who wants to read it. This entire process felt like a dream to which I never wanted to wake from. I feel as though because of BookLeaf Publishing, I can expose my vulnerable self and show others who may feel similarly that it's alright to have emotions and to ask for help. I encourage anyone who is struggling to reach out, because you and your feelings are valid and important. Thank you.

PREFACE

My story is told through the words on the pages. Many battles thrown my way. Some I've conquered and others I'm still learning to overcome.

I always believed I could overcome my problems alone. Years of trying to win internal battles led me to wrong paths and unhealthy coping mechanisms. Coping strategies that I am still trying to stop and find safer and healthier ways to deal with my emotions and feelings.

No battles are easy to overcome. There are better days ahead and I want to experience them, so I keep fighting. I hope anyone who is struggling will keep fighting too. Baby steps to better days are crucial. Don't be hard on yourself when you take two steps back. Rushing to heal our minds won't have the same effect as taking it slow and a step at a time.

Each poem is a part of my story. A piece of myself. Every page is filled with honesty and vulnerability. No poem was particularly difficult to write, unlike actually admitting to myself how real it is.

Now in your palms are pages of vulnerability and raw emotion. Turn each page to unlock more of this mind. Maybe this mind is relatable and a realisation that the holder of this book is not alone.

Upside Down

I'm waiting to die.
Metaphorically my mind is already dead.
I'm just waiting for my body to catch up.

Isn't it funny?
As in the way I used to feel,
Is the way I wish I could feel now.

Ups and downs,
Highs and lows.
Angles are deceiving,
Depending on your position.
To the eye a frown is sad,
But if the sorrowed being were to do a
handstand - an illusion of happiness appears.
Our brains can skip the logic,
That our eyes only show so much perception.
Forgetting when a frown is flipped,
It imitates a smile.
However, the other features are on the wrong
side.
Reminding us that the upside down human,
With the upside down smile,
Is nothing but sad.
When nothing is happy,
In her upside down life.

Does a four leaf clover still hold value,
If it's plucked and left with three?
A once treasured find,
No longer cherished once damaged and broken.

Comforting Routine

Fresh pyjamas,
Crisp, new bedding,
And a heated shower.
Comfort.

Ignite a candlewick,
Dim the lights,
While steady chords float in the air.
Comfort.

My door stays closed,
But my curtains remain withdrawn,
To let the moon watch over me.
Comfort.

Slide into bed,
Stuffed bear underarm,
A glass half full on my bedside table.
Comfort.

Layers of pillows,
Electric fan spinning with a hum,
As the gentle breeze soothes me.
Comfort.

Music remains flowing,
To silence my tears,
While I greet my dreams with a damp pillow.
Routine.

I Try

I try to be someone that's worthy,
I try to be someone that's great.
I try to be someone they're proud of,
But I'm just a mistake.

I try to be someone that's needed,
And I try to be a stranger who cares.
I try so hard to be what they dreamed I'd be,
But I'm not and they know it.

I try to be someone that's happy,
I try to be someone who's carefree.
I try to fit in because to them different is a sin,
I'm just trying to not be me.

Bottle It

I feel so much,
Trying not to let it show.
I don't want to be the problem,
They say that I am.

I once voiced how I felt,
My emotions quickly shot down.
They said I had no reason to feel that way,
So I stopped speaking out.

Now when I feel something,
I don't let it show till I'm alone.
I have no reason to feel like this,
Even if I did that's not what people want to hear.

Yet if I don't keep it in,
While everyone's around.
I'll just be making a fuss,
Now I bottle it till I've bottled enough.

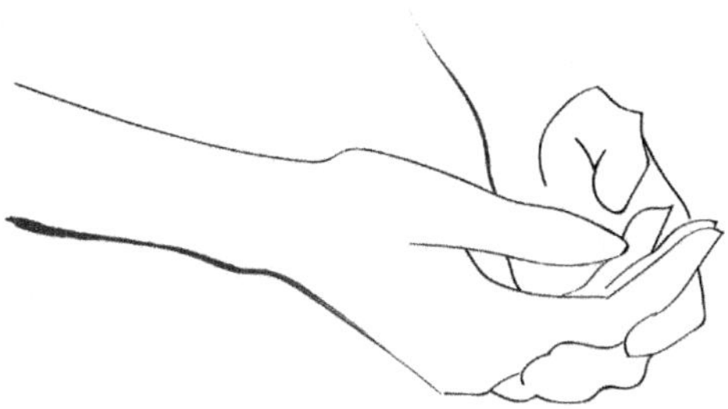

Writing With Silver

I write with silver, and it turns red.

Silver pen,
Captivating beauty of my deadly friend.
The sharpness of her edges,
She's with me beginning to end.

Cream paper,
Areas left scarred and torn from the silver pen's touch.
She can paint over the existing art on my paper,
Nowhere is too damaged - at least nowhere too much.

Red ink.
The silver pen marks my cream paper but red ink flows,
For a brief moment my beating heart froze.
But when the silver pen's art fades and slowly goes,
The uncontrollable need for my deadly friend burns stronger and grows.

I write with silver and it turns red.

I crave her touch to take my pain.
I write with silver and it turns red.
I need her touch to silence my brain.

Back when I wrote with silver till it turned red,
Now I write with silver until I'm …

Skull With No Key

Stuck in my head,
No comfort in their voices.
Escape is non-existent,
Impossible to mute their words.

Trapped in the maze of my brain,
Forever going in loops like a broken record.
The louder they shout,
The weaker I feel.

Caged in my mind,
No one can pull me out from the darkness that swallows me.
It feels like I'm in a glass box,
With people on the outside watching me suffocate.

Imprisoned with my thoughts,
Barred up and completely locked in.
No knight in shining armour can free me,
From being haunted by myself.
Until I meet my grave,
I live in a skull with no key.

How Should I Feel?

Should I feel confused?
I am - but can I?
Maybe I should feel disgusted,
And sorry too.

Even after so long,
You moved on.
Found 'her',
Who wasn't me.
That broke me,
More than it should have.
I felt that sinking sensation,
My heart dropping with the tears that ran.
The meals prepared,
But no energy left to swallow.

Heartache is real,
And I felt it.
Others say, "You're being dramatic. You barely knew each other",
But I was never shown an ounce of love by anyone before.
No one stayed long enough to see the real me,
You did though.
Learned my flaws, insecurities and past,

And still you stuck around.
Built my confidence and unbricked my walls,
Gave all I had to you thinking it was enough.
Thinking I was enough,
How wrong I really was.

There's a part that baffles me,
And I don't yet understand.
Even though you have 'her',
You still reach out to me.
I don't mean cliché small talk,
But the regret you seem to show from the choices you made.

How am I supposed to feel about that?
How would 'she' feel?
I wonder but also doubt,
If 'she' is aware of the connection we still share.
How would I feel if I were in 'her' six-inch heels?
I know out of girl coded respect I should cut this tie,
But it's tougher to slice when the person you're losing saved your life.
My lifeline is both my saviour and my kryptonite.

House Without The Home

Four walls made of brick,
Sheltered from the outside world.
But these four walls,
Hold no power when protecting me from the
inside.

Silence within these four walls,
Never surpasses the five minute mark.
When the time is up,
Chaos breaks loose.

Those who should be my guardians,
Turn their swords against each other.
With venomous words and plates being tossed
like grenades,
My body shuts down while I'm caught in the
crossfire.

When the battlefield is abandoned,
All that remains is shattered glass.
As I stand and make no move to flee,
The breath that I've been holding can finally be
released.

These four walls made of brick,
Shield me from the beasts out the door.
But these four walls made of brick,
Are home to the two beasts that live on the
inside.

I live in a house made of brick,
But I can't rest easy.
I feel no safety within these four walls,
This is a house without the home.

Wasted On The High

Woke up on the wrong side of the bed again,
Rubbed my eyes and brushed my hair again,
Left the house and went about my daily routine,
Nothing ever seems to change and I'm tearing at the seams.
Don't you know its getting harder?

Don't be fooled it's not easy,
Being someone that's like me,
I'm living in a darkened world,
And here I am all alone,
In my cold and empty home,
But I'm wasted on the high again.

Another night just like the one before,
Pull the blinds and lock the bedroom door,
I raise my sleeves and bring out my metallic friend,
I close my eyes and I wait for the pain to end,
Can't you see it's getting harder?

And here I am all alone,
In my cold and empty home,
Still I'm living on the high again,

And can't you see, it's not easy,
Being someone that's like me,
And I'm wasted on the high again.

All I need is someone to call me,
All I need is someone to hold me.
I need someone to save me from myself,
Cause I'm not strong enough to ask for help.
Wasted on the high.

Under Their Eyes

I feel the stare of their judging eyes,
Following every step I take.
They spare no blink with their fixated eyes,
Awaiting my next indefinite mistake.

Just me and these predatory eyes,
You'd think in company I'd feel at home.
But the truth is plain when surrounded by eyes,
I've never quite felt more alone.

The hawks watch me with their unforgiving eyes,
Preying on me each time I miss the mark.
Only my neon flaws tracked by their burning eyes,
Now I try to stay hidden from sight by locking myself in the dark.

Invisible Hands

I still feel those invisible hands,
The way they touched whatever they pleased.
No words could block the path they roamed,
They were the parasite that infested my body.

I still feel those invisible hands,
They haunt my dreams in the night.
Now I fear they are all like you,
A parasite that feasts upon my mind.

I still feel those invisible hands,
When all I'm wearing is my skin.
Virtually impossible to erase the permanent
marks you left,
You are the parasitic devil that stole my
innocence.

Sleepwalk Living

To the girl who spends her spare time catching up on sleep,
Even though she gets the nine hours each night.
I know how you feel,
Sleep is where you are most at peace.

It's exhausting spending each waking minute,
Feeling as though nothing is real.
As if stuck in a simulator,
That's caught in a repetitive glitch.

When your head hits the pillow,
The world is paused.
It's almost a joke,
That she feels more alive in her own dreams.

So when her eyes open next,
All she thinks about is when they will close again.
It's the vicious cycle,
Of sleepwalk living.

One Glass

It's been a long month,
I'll just have one.
Glass filled up with the burning taste,
That left a trail of fire down my throat.
But now I feel lighter,
Perhaps this beverage will make me feel
brighter.

It's been a rough week,
Just one glass or two.
Desperate to drown my thoughts with a sip,
But one glass full turned to one bottle empty.
At first, I felt better,
Now I may have drunk too much.
All I wanted was to easily seek,
A way to relieve the stresses of my week.

It's been an intense day,
I'll just have one glass and then I'll rest.
Now hunting for my toxic drip,
Wanting anything to blur my graphic mind.
But after raiding all the cupboards,
Not a drop left to be found.
I look at dozens of bottles in my green boxes on
the curb,

Thinking maybe this bitter spirit has a lethal
hold on me.
I try to resist but the urge is too strong,
Now I race down to the store to buy what I need
but know is wrong.

Failed System

"Hold your breath,
Count to ten.
Breathe out slowly,
Well done - you're cured."

So, I hold my breath,
Until I can't anymore.
It didn't end my suffering,
Try again - you failed.

The system is flawed,
They say to reach out for help if you need it.
But you're let down when you do,
By being added to the forever growing waiting list.

"Run a bath,
Try to relax.
Soak in the warmth,
Well done - you're cured"

I ran the bath,
For my watery grave.
But my body surfaced for air,
Try again - you failed.

You do need professional help,
That's why you're on their list.
They know you're sick,
Just not enough to get immediate help to prevent it from escalating.

“Have a cup of tea,
Brew it nice and hot.
Sit now and have a sip,
Well done - you’re cured”

I boiled the kettle,
But not for a cup of tea.
Poured the scolding water upon my skin,
Try again - you failed.

By the time you reach the top of their list,
You're a shell of the person you were.
Many months and likely years have passed in that time,
No doubt you're on their urgent list now.

“Get out the house and take a walk,
The fresh air will work wonders.
Each step forward is a good sign,
Well done - you’re cured.”

I left the house,

Now I'm at a cliff side.
They said, "each step forward is a good sign".
Now it's you who failed.

The severity of your mental health,
Should not prevent you from getting support when you ask.
The list would not be growing as fast as the population,
If help was offered from the beginning.
Changes need to be made,
To stop the failed system from failing anyone else.

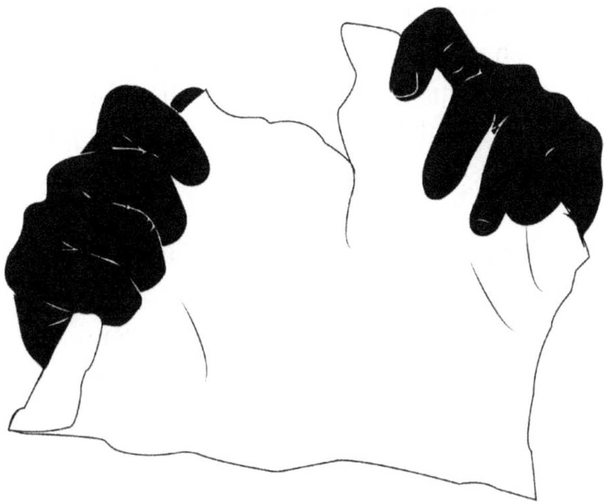

Dream-Reality Confusion

I think I'm going crazy,
My brain is plotting things against me.
Memories have been altered and switched,
I think neurologically there's a glitch.

When I close my eyes and start to dream,
The story gets muddled with my daily routine.
Things I should find easy to know,
If it's real or a dream but no.

I woke up this morning calling for my sister,
But when I got no answer I think that I've missed her.
My parents question whom I'm calling for,
But when I tell them they think I'm joking for sure.

I'm confused and don't get how this makes any sense,
It's getting scary and I'm feeling more tense.
I thought for certain I could ace my family tree,
But I can't tell a dream from reality.

Shoes On My Feet, Apple On The Tree, Duck In A Pond

Sometimes I imagine if they were in my shoes,
How would they walk?
When I try to step it feels like rocks are weighing me down,
But they tell me to deal with it and be grateful for having shoes at all.

They say, "The apple doesn't fall far from the tree",
As if I share something with them that connects us to the core.
But all I feel we share is blood,
And less so like I'm the apple that belongs in their tree.

Our views are so different,
But mine are always wrong.
Just reminded I'm unworthy,
The ugly duckling in their pond.

I often imagine,
That if I lived alone.
It would be audibly quieter but not different,
Because I'd still be on my own.

Take Me Now

I can't keep acting this happy part,
Exhaustion is draining my body to the max.
When they say, "Tired eyes reflect tired hearts",
That's nothing but facts.

So, take me now,
I want to go.
Take me now,
I have no home.

The struggle to leave my bed is real,
Wishing I never woke up at all.
I can't find the words for how I feel,
So I stay hidden while building my wall.

So, take me now,
I'm too tired to keep trying.
Take me now,
I'm not afraid of dying.

My brain was fogged at 2 A.M last night,
Surrounded by darkness and shadows that loom.
I wasn't ready to lose my fight,
So I drove down to the emergency room.

So, take me soon but not just yet,
It's not my time to go.
Take me soon but not just yet,
When it's time to go I'll know.

Weather Maker

How a Weather Maker feels,
Is something like this...

Do you know how it feels,
To have your emotions consume you in every way?

From happiness feeling like euphoria,
Or anger feeling like you're seeing red.

Fear turns to blood stilled panic,
And sadness is like you have nothing left.

They rise within like a flash flood,
And overflow like a blocked drain.

There's no halting the waves,
They leave a scene of destruction wherever they go.

Eventually the storm stills,
But when the Weather Maker looks back.

They see the pain they've caused,
And the guilt clouds overhead.

The drizzle won't end,
Until the sorrow passes.

Waiting for a friend,
To bring the Weather Maker's sun out again.

No One Speaks

No one speaks about the unattractive side of
mental health.
When the last time you brushed your teeth or
showered.
How long ago was it that you smiled?
Rephrase - smiled and meant it?

No one speaks about the energy you lack to
clean your room,
They just accuse you of being lazy.
Your social life is effort and draining,
So you cut connections but end up labelled the
bad friend.

No one speaks about the ugly side of mental
health.
Where your long sleeves, pill stash and isolation
is all you know.
It's all, "Mental health matters",
Until symptoms are attention seeking because
it's not their romanticised version anymore.

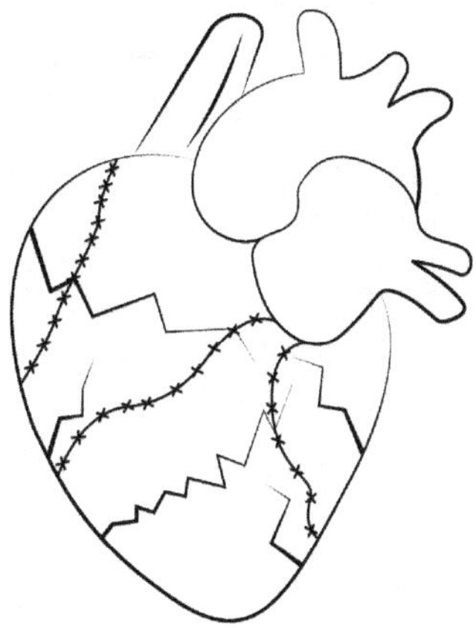

The Ending

Standing before the mirror,
But not sure who I see.
There's just an empty soul,
Staring back at me.

Her hair desperately needs a brush,
And her teeth are in long need of a clean.
She looks so defeated,
Unlike anyone I've seen.

Her eyes meet mine,
Forces a smile that's fake.
Her dam breaks as tears flow,
She knows it's too late.

She takes one last glance,
Then exits the bathroom.
Stand high upon the chair,
And looks up to the moon.

Her fate is in her hands,
Desperate to leave this world.
The rope scarfed around her neck,
A "Let down" is all she's ever been told.

As she takes her final breath,
While looking out at the moon.
She gave in and let go,
Relieved it will all be over soon.

Remember This

When stuck at rock bottom,
And you feel you're out of luck.
Remember when you're down there,
The only way to go is up.

On the journey to recovery,
It's not a race so bear in mind.
Don't compare yourself to others,
Just take it one day at a time.

If you have a bad day,
That leaves you reaching for the knife.
Please always try to remember,
It's a bad day - not a bad life.

www.ingramcontent.com/pod-product-compliance
Lightning Source LLC
Chambersburg PA
CBHW051738130826
49812CB00033B/906
* 9 7 8 9 3 5 7 2 1 0 3 0 0 *